PRACTICE HEARING GOD'S VOICE

Daily Devotional Journal

A Practical 7-Day Devotional, Meditation,
Journalling, Affirmation, and Prayer for
Knowing God's Voice

Volume I

Printed in the United States of America.

ISBN: 978-1-958404-96-6 (paperback)

PREFACE

Isaiah 60-61 and Joel 2 are two of my favourite texts of Scripture. Both are prophetic and speak of ages to come. There is a possibility that we have already stepped into those ages. While I believe in the glorious and radiant emergence of the church, I believe that she must come forth out of chaos. As it was in the beginning, so shall it be in the end. The earth was formless and void, and darkness was on the face of the earth. Then the light that God is broke forth and created order and beauty from the chaos.

As we are submerged into a world of chaos and darkness spreading across the world, the light that we are will break forth. The Bible speaks of a time when men's hearts will fail from fear. Our only hope of emerging from this chaos in all our magnificent glory is to increase our capacity to hear God's voice. Our capacity to hear God is vital in the times we now live and in the ages to come. It is as vital now as it was in Biblical times when ordinary men and women of God did extraordinary things because of their capacity to hear and obey the voice of God.

All creation is sustained by the Word of God. If God stops speaking for only a milli-second, creation would cease to exist. Most Christians are either unable to clearly identify God's voice or do not know how to differentiate the voice of God from all other voices.

This practical daily devotional journal was designed to address the importance of us hearing God when He speaks. Hearing God is a practice that leads to a state of being. No one can truly become a master without practice. "But solid food belongs to those who are of full age, that is, those who by reason of use have their senses exercised to discern both good and evil." (Hebrews 5:14). When we learn to hear God and obey the instructions given, we will begin to manifest the will, heart, and mind of God in creation, even amid chaos.

HOW TO USE THIS DEVOTIONAL JOURNAL

First, I share a text of Scripture along with my personal thoughts and interpretation. You don't have to agree with my theology; I have a rather unconventional 21st-century perspective on Scripture. What is important is your own takeaway and the conclusions you draw for yourself after examining the facts and reflecting on Scripture as a whole.

Our individual journeys are unique, and we will form our own personal theological interpretations based on our backgrounds, what we have been taught, what we have experienced, and the level we are at in our walk with God.

Next is a meditation. This practice helps establish a proper posture to hear God. Pay attention to two things: visual (what you see in your imagination/mind) and audible (what you hear).

Journal what you have seen and heard.

Finally, affirmations are included to be spoken audibly. You should hear yourself speaking these affirmations for maximum results. On many occasions, King David had to speak to his soul. This practice helps shift us from feeding from the tree of the knowledge of good and evil to feeding from the tree of life.

May this practical tool aid in your daily devotion and walk with God as we practice hearing God together, so, like Jesus, we learn to only do what we see our Father doing and say what we hear our Father saying.

In addition to the readings, meditations, and prayers, you can also incorporate communion.

TABLE OF CONTENTS

DAY ONE

PASSING THROUGH THE FIRE

Simon, Simon (Peter), listen! Satan has asked excessively that [all of] you be given up to him [out of the power and keeping of God], that he might sift [all of] you like grain, But I have prayed especially for you [Peter], that your [own] faith may not fail; and when you yourself have turned again, strengthen and establish your brethren. (Luke 22:31-32 - AMPC).

A few years ago, the climax of the church age brought to the forefront what we know today as the prosperity gospel. Along with that came the belief that a believer is supposed to walk in perpetual prosperity and not suffer. We were conditioned to think that saying yes to Jesus would excuse us from suffering. I remember several altar calls on my side of the world where it was said, "Come to Jesus, and He will fix everything." Any serious Bible scholar will see the flaw in this belief.

Consider the life of Job. Unbeknownst to him, a conversation took place in an ethereal realm concerning his life and commitment to God. The adversary was given permission to afflict Job with one exception: spare his life. Fast forward to the text where Jesus speaks to Peter and tells him, essentially, that permission has been granted for him to be tested. Jesus never prayed that Peter would be spared from the test but that his faith would not fail. Somehow, through what Peter was about to endure, he would experience growth or further solidifying of his faith to the point where he could encourage others.

A part of our faith journey is to pass through the fire. Our walk with God is not one of perpetual paradise with a pristine background and a nice, orange sunset. While that is a beautiful scene, the faith walk is often on a very dark, rugged path with thorns and tests designed not to destroy us but to strengthen us. Jesus intercedes for us, not that we will always be spared from the adversary's attempts to diminish our faith, but that our faith remains resolute. David said we will face many troubles in this life, but the Lord will deliver us from them all (see Psalm 34:19).

There can only be one of two outcomes with every fiery trial that we face in this life: either our faith fails or it remains resolute. When your day of testing comes, may your faith not fail.

MEDITATION

Be still, and know that I am God; (Psalm 46:10a - NKJV).

In stillness, God is known. He is heard by those who listen. He is seen by those who look for Him.

Close your eyes for a few moments and think about the last few days. Reflect on the difficulties you faced, the times you were on the road, and the moments when you had to find something to eat. Ask this question in your mind: *"Lord, where were You as I went through these days?"* Be open to Him answering you by showing you His hand in your life during those times. It might have been near misses on the road, a call that encouraged you, or someone helping you in some way. The idea is to begin to identify God's movement and interaction in your daily life.

Spend about 15-30 minutes on this, then journal your thoughts as you come back from this meditation.

WHAT DID THE LORD SHOW YOU?

_____

_____

_____

WHAT DID THE LORD SAY TO YOU?

AFFIRMATION

I decree and declare that in the midst of my test, my faith remains strong and resolute. I believe God will bring me through this. I am more than a conqueror through Christ Jesus.

PRAYER

Father, someone said that when life gives me a lemon, I should make lemonade. How easy it is to lose faith in a time when faith is needed the most. We often believe the lies of the adversary, who comes to deceive us into doubting Your Word. But today, I choose to remain resolute in my faith, even in the midst of my fiery trials. Life gets hard. People disappoint. Unexpected circumstances creep up on us from time to time. One after another, we receive reports of bad news, and it is so easy to sink into complacency and believe that You have forsaken this world. But I choose to believe You. I choose to remain steadfast in my faith. I choose to believe Your report. I am healed. I am free. I am strong. I am more than a conqueror, for You have strengthened me and made me an overcomer by the blood of Jesus Christ. Amen.

DAY TWO

CHILD-LIKE FAITH

But He said, Leave the children alone! Allow the little ones to come to Me, and do not forbid or restrain or hinder them, for of such [as these] is the kingdom of heaven composed. (Matthew 19:14 - AMPC).

Comprehending the enigma concealed within this text is fundamental to our spiritual journey. Simply observing a child enables us to understand what Jesus was saying. A degree of trustworthiness and innocence exists in the way an infant reacts to the outside world. They are receptive to what is said and lack any basis for skepticism. They are not preoccupied with matters such as where their next meal will come from, how they will get to school, how they will stay warm at night, or anything else. Children embrace each moment with all their being and take pleasure in life. They derive joy from the simplest pleasures and are unburdened by concerns, doubts, and uncertainties regarding the future.

Furthermore, children have no difficulty accepting what they cannot perceive. As one ages, it is believed that concerns, doubts, and all other negative characteristics are acquired. Typically, children are more candid about the truth than adults. David said, "You will show me the path of life; in Your presence is fullness of joy, at Your right hand there are pleasures forevermore." (Psalm 16:11 – AMPC). An infant is more receptive to delights and joys than an adult acting to the best of their intellect. While Jesus was on earth, children flocked to Him, whereas adults viewed Him with skepticism.

This analogy regarding the kingdom of God being composed of child-like individuals has multiple levels of significance. An infant exhibits reliance and trust. They are completely dependent on their parents for sustenance, direction, and protection. Similarly, we must place our trust in our heavenly Father. An infant also exhibits qualities of purity and modesty. The development of hubris, cynicism, and skepticism that occurs with maturation rarely affects children. A child is receptive to instruction. They consistently strive for knowledge and never adopt the stance of possessing all knowledge. Children are untainted by the complexity of faith. They hold their beliefs without the intricate reservations and doubts that are commonly present in adults.

As we strive to become acquainted with the practicalities of God's kingdom, let us adopt the disposition of children, for we are all children of our Father regardless of our age.

MEDITATION

Let us then fearlessly, confidently, and boldly draw near to the throne of grace (the throne of God's unmerited favor to us sinners), that we may receive mercy for our failures and find grace to help in good time for every need—appropriate help and well-timed help, coming just when we need it. (Hebrews 4:16 - AMPC).

A child is always welcome in the Father's house, so let's pay our Father a visit. Close your eyes for a few moments and think about the throne room. There are several descriptions in the Bible that we can use to engage our imagination. For this meditation, we will use Revelation 4:

After these things I looked, and behold, a door standing open in heaven. And the first voice which I heard was like a trumpet speaking with me, saying, "Come up here, and I will show you things which must take place after this." Immediately I was in the Spirit; and behold, a throne set in heaven, and One sat on the throne. And He who sat

there was like a jasper and a sardius stone in appearance; and there was a rainbow around the throne, in appearance like an emerald. Around the throne were twenty-four thrones, and on the thrones I saw twenty-four elders sitting, clothed in white robes; and they had crowns of gold on their heads. And from the throne proceeded lightnings, thunderings, and voices. Seven lamps of fire were burning before the throne, which are the seven Spirits of God. Before the throne there was a sea of glass, like crystal. And in the midst of the throne, and around the throne, were four living creatures full of eyes in front and in back. The first living creature was like a lion, the second living creature like a calf, the third living creature had a face like a man, and the fourth living creature was like a flying eagle. The four living creatures, each having six wings, were full of eyes around and within. And they do not rest day or night, saying: "Holy, holy, holy, Lord God Almighty, Who was and is and is to come!" (Revelation 4:1-8 - NKJV).

Spend about 15-30 minutes with this, then journal your thoughts as you come back from this meditation.

WHAT DID THE LORD SHOW YOU?

_____

_____

_____

_____

_____

_____

_____

_____

_____

_____

_____

_____

_____

_____

_____

_____

_____

_____

_____

_____

_____

_____

WHAT DID THE LORD SAY TO YOU?

AFFIRMATION

I decree and declare that I have child-like faith. I trust God to provide, sustain, protect, and guide me through this day. I am teachable and always learning. I am open to God's interaction and engagement in my life today. I hear His voice, and I obey His instructions.

PRAYER

Father, it can be difficult to differentiate Your voice from all the other voices in the world, but I believe there is a distinct quality to Your voice as You speak. Thank You for the written Word of God that guides me in this process. As I read and meditate on Your Word, help me to remember. Open my imagination to see as men and women who have walked in the Spirit are able to describe what they saw. I accept Your invitation to "Come up higher." I accept Your invitation to walk with You in the cool of the evening. I choose to sit at Your feet and learn from You. Amen.

DAY THREE

RELEASING THE TEMPORARY FOR THE ETERNAL

Jesus answered him, if you would be perfect [that is, have that spiritual maturity which accompanies self-sacrificing character], go and sell what you have and give to the poor, and you will have riches in heaven; and come, be My disciple [side with My party and follow Me]. (Matthew 19:21 - NKJV).

Sometimes the very thing we attach ourselves to and think we cannot do without is the thing that hinders us from coming into the fullness of what God created us to be. There is a spiritual law that in order to keep something, we must be willing to lose it.

For whoever desires to save his life will lose it, but whoever loses his life for My sake will find it. For what profit is it to a man if he gains the whole world, and loses his own soul? Or what will a man give in exchange for his soul? (Matthew 16:25-26 - NKJV).

To gain, we must lose. Such a strange paradox to embrace in our times, and it is the reason the disciples of Christ could not understand His mission to die, even though it was explained to them.

It is believed that Abraham was tested ten times. Some say it was seven. Regardless of what the figure is, what is important is the last test. Abraham was told to sacrifice his one and only son. I imagine the difficulty with this command is that Isaac was the son of promise. Abraham waited a few decades for Isaac to be born. There are many schools of thought as to what caused the delay, but the one I have accepted is that Abraham needed to be prepared. Isaac was the central focus of God keeping His promise to make Abraham into a great nation. The death of Isaac would have left God's promise unfulfilled, yet we are talking about the God of the impossible.

According to Hebrews:

By faith Abraham, when he was put to the test [while the testing of his faith was still in progress], had already brought Isaac for an offering; he who had gladly received and welcomed [God's] promises was ready to sacrifice his only son, of whom it was said, Through Isaac shall your descendants be reckoned. For he reasoned that

God was able to raise [him] up even from among the dead. Indeed in the sense that Isaac was figuratively dead [potentially sacrificed], he did [actually] receive him back from the dead. (Hebrews 11:17-19 - AMPC).

Abraham believed something he had never seen: that God could raise the dead. The test that we go through in life will provoke us to believe in something we have never seen. It requires us to take God at His Word. The rich young ruler could not part with his earthly wealth, even though there was a promise in the Words of Jesus of something even better: riches in heaven. At that moment, he made a choice: he rejected what he could not see in favour of what he could see.

Most, if not all, Biblical writers at some point surrendered the temporal to embrace an eternal reality. At some point in our journey of faith, we will be asked to do the same thing.

MEDITATION

He who loves father or mother more than Me is not worthy of Me. And he who loves son or daughter more than Me is not worthy of Me. And he who does not take his cross and follow after Me is not worthy of Me. He who finds his life will lose it, and

he who loses his life for My sake will find it. (Matthew 10:37-39 - NKJV).

As we meditate on this Scripture, let's do a simple meditation. Close your eyes and begin to examine your life. Look at all that you possess, your family, your circle of friends, your career; everything that makes you YOU. Now ask yourself this question: *"Am I willing to give it all up for God?"* Give an honest answer. Anything in your life that may seem hard to surrender completely to God can become a hindrance to your spiritual ascendancy.

Spend about 15-30 minutes with this, then journal your thoughts as you come back from this meditation.

WHAT DID THE LORD SHOW YOU?

_____

_____

_____

_____

_____

_____

_____

_____

WHAT DID THE LORD SAY TO YOU?

_____

_____

_____

_____

_____

_____

_____

_____

_____

_____

_____

_____

_____

_____

_____

_____

_____

_____

_____

_____

_____

AFFIRMATION

I decree and declare that I am born from above. I have the DNA of my Father in heaven. As Jesus is, so am I on the earth. I am willing to let go of everything that hinders my growth in God.

PRAYER

Father, I have examined my life, all my possessions and the people within my circle, and this is my honest assessment. (Share your assessment with God). These are the areas I struggle to surrender completely to You (Share those areas. Be open and honest). God, I want nothing to hinder me from becoming all You created me to be. I know that my possessions and the people in my life are gifts from You. As Job said, You have the power to give, and You have the power to take away. I know there is a price to pay to follow You completely, and I am willing. Am I able? I honestly don't know, but there is nothing I cannot do without Your help. Equip me as You align me to my divine purpose. Amen.

DAY FOUR

THE POWER OF FAITH

Now in the morning, as He returned to the city, He was hungry. And seeing a fig tree by the road, He came to it and found nothing on it but leaves, and said to it, "Let no fruit grow on you ever again." Immediately the fig tree withered away. And when the disciples saw it, they marveled, saying, "How did the fig tree wither away so soon?" (Matthew 21:18-20 - NKJV).

Could this world have survived humanity if everything we said manifested? In an age of gossip and anxiety, I would say no. It is a power we have intrinsically, but God has somehow truncated that power for our own survival. It is a good thing that we don't always experience the reality that we frame with our words.

I have always marvelled at certain scriptures. For one:

So Jesus answered and said to them, "Assuredly, I say to you, if you have faith and do not doubt, you will not only do what was done to the fig tree, but

also if you say to this mountain, 'Be removed and be cast into the sea,' it will be done. And whatever things you ask in prayer, believing, you will receive." (Matthew 21:21-22 - NKJV).

There is power in our faith to frame realities. Jesus said, *"Whatever things you ask in prayer, believing, you will receive."* That is a tall order that cannot be minimized through our lack of experience or hermeneutics. I believe it means what it says, even if that is not our immediate experience. If we are unable, with our words, to manifest our faith, then there is a reason for that. It's not that the Scriptures need to be reinterpreted. I believe this power to speak and see the reality of what was spoken is embedded in our maturity as a son of God. The believer inherits the power that is God at his/her spiritual rebirth (born again), but the fullness of that power is not fully experienced until that child becomes a son. The question then becomes, *"How do we mature our souls? What are the practices we need to engage in consistently that will increase our level of maturity?"* This is where spiritual practices are important.

There are different levels and dimensions to every spiritual practice. This is why the Bible says:

For in it the righteousness of God is revealed from faith to faith; as it is written, "The just shall live by faith." (Roman 1:17 - NKJV).

This Scripture can easily be interpreted as *"from one level of faith to another level of faith."* I like using the education system as an example of spiritual growth. No student remains at the same grade, unless something is wrong with their capacity to learn. Each grade is higher than the last, and continues upward until one attains a doctorate. There is nothing higher, so once you hit that mark, you have only to acquire multiple doctorates, but there is no level that is higher than that. It works a little differently for faith as I believe the levels are infinite.

Where we want to get is that place where, like Jesus said, we can speak to a mountain and see it uprooted and cast into the sea. This is possible.

MEDITATION

For with God nothing will be impossible. (Luke 1:37 - NKJV).

As we meditate on this Scripture, let's do a simple meditation. Close your eyes and turn your gaze inward. God lives in you. What does this mean? What does that feel like? Is God moving inside our bodies?

Is He seated on a throne in our hearts? How does God live inside us? Personalize it! *What does this mean for me that God lives in me? How am I the temple of the Holy Spirit? If God lives in me, and nothing is impossible for Him, is there anything impossible for me?*

Spend about 15-30 minutes with this, then journal your thoughts as you come back from this meditation.

WHAT DID THE LORD SHOW YOU?

_____

_____

_____

_____

_____

_____

_____

_____

_____

_____

_____

_____

_____

WHAT DID THE LORD SAY TO YOU?

_____

_____

_____

_____

_____

_____

_____

_____

_____

_____

_____

_____

_____

_____

_____

_____

_____

_____

_____

_____

_____

_____

_____

AFFIRMATION

I have faith to declare a thing and see it established. I have faith to walk on water. I have faith to speak to mountains and see them removed. I have faith to heal the sick and raise the dead.

PRAYER

Father, the mystery of the human being becoming a believer and becoming the temple where You dwell is beyond my understanding, but Your Word says that is who I am. I am the temple of the Holy Spirit. I accept this reality and believe it is true because You said it, and You cannot lie. I ask that You, Lord, help me to understand this reality, and to know what it really means to be a dwelling place for You. Teach me how to walk out this reality in my own life. Amen.

DAY FIVE

LIFE IN DEATH

And as it is appointed for men to die once, but after this the judgment, so Christ was offered once to bear the sins of many. To those who eagerly wait for Him He will appear a second time, apart from sin, for salvation. (Hebrews 9:27-28 - NKJV).

I recently attended the funeral service for one of my church mothers. She was one of a kind and was labeled a "legend" in her own right for the myriads of contributions she made to society, the church, and the community. She was indeed a stalwart, and if I should dedicate this small book to anyone, it would be in her memory. She was a master English teacher and an avid church worker who couldn't get enough to do, and she sacrificed many hours of sleep to get the work done. I had known her pretty much all my life, and unsurprisingly, it was one funeral of many that I had to find a corner and cry.

Some years ago, the Lord told me that if I was going to live, I must deal with the reality of death, and so I have. Death has shocked me to the core, from young friends, classmates, neighbors, and family members (including my father), this painful reality is unavoidable for the living, and I have not experienced the worst in terms of trauma as some others. I have developed a hatred for death, and knowing that the people we know and love are saved and in a better place does not always ease the pain.

When it comes to hearing God, I am sure we have all been there. What is God saying in these moments of pain and trauma? When someone we know has been ripped from our lives, and we have to watch them being buried beneath the ground? I have heard the painful screams of those who have watched this unfolding before their very eyes, and at some point, we have all been there.

Why is death so painful?

Jesus wept when His friend Lazarus died, even though He knew He was going to raise him from the dead. Jesus didn't weep when His cousin, John, was beheaded. Neither was John raised back to life. It is sometimes hard to fathom God's ways and thoughts, but the truth is that He sees the bigger picture. Heaven's perspective of death is not the same as ours because we operate from a fallen consciousness that often lacks enlightenment, so it is a daily struggle to see beyond the reality of this dark world to the truth of the world of Light where life is multi-faceted and multi-dimensional. Death takes us from here to there, and while we often want everyone we love to remain on this side of life, the ultimate goal of our journey is really to get to the other side; some will go before us, and, hopefully, not all of us will have to walk through the jaws of death.

Behold, I tell you a mystery: We shall not all sleep, but we shall all be changed—in a moment, in the twinkling of an eye, at the last trumpet. For the trumpet will sound, and the dead will be raised incorruptible, and we shall be changed. (1 Corinthians 15:51-52 - NKJV).

The one encouragement I can give you now is that death is not the end. It is a gloriously new beginning, and there is a distinction between the dead and the living.

But concerning the dead, that they rise, have you not read in the book of Moses, in the burning bush passage, how God spoke to him, saying, 'I am the God of Abraham, the God of Isaac, and the God of Jacob'? He is not the God of the dead, but the God of the living. (Mark 12:26-27 - NKJV).

I personally believe there are many saints who have died who are actually not in the grave. But don't quote me on that.

MEDITATION

For You will not leave my soul in Sheol, nor will You allow Your Holy One to see corruption. (Psalm 16:10 - NKJV).

This Scripture is often attributed to Jesus, but I believe it also applies to us who are engrafted into Christ. As we meditate on this Scripture, let's do a simple meditation. Close your eyes and consider the reality of death. Think about those you have lost, the circumstances surrounding the loss, and how you felt. Don't try to process your feelings, but become acutely aware that God is with you, and He is feeling what you are feeling. God lives in you. He knows pain. He knows death. He knows loss, trauma, and suffering. He knows what you are feeling. Now (and this will be difficult for many), think about your own death and the empty space that will be left behind when you are no longer here. Process that reality for a minute, then force your mind to think beyond that. See yourself from an eternal perspective: your pre-creation existence when you were in the mind of God shouting for joy as creation emerged. Know with absolute certainty that because you are here now, you will never cease to exist and shed your fear of death that causes so many to experience different levels of anxiety.

Spend about 15-30 minutes with this, then journal your thoughts as you come back from this meditation.

WHAT DID THE LORD SHOW YOU?

_____

_____

_____

_____

_____

_____

_____

_____

_____

_____

_____

_____

_____

_____

_____

_____

WHAT DID THE LORD SAY TO YOU?

AFFIRMATION

I have life, and I have it more abundantly. I will feed on the body and blood of Jesus, and by so doing, I will access His life, His nature, His blood, His DNA. I will live and not die to declare the words of the Lord in the land of the living. My life is eternal.

PRAYER

Father, death and dying is a painful and sometimes scary reality, and among the living, we really don't want to think about it, and we struggle to accept it at times. Help us, Lord, not to shy away from something so real and so often necessary in our walk through life. We age, we lose our vitality and strength, and though our souls are renewed each day, our bodies sometimes deteriorate so much that they can no longer hold our eternal selves. Lord, we make bad choices with what we feed our bodies and how we care for this, the temple of the Holy Spirit. Forgive us. Help us to make better choices with food, and commit to caring for this temple where you live. Bless us with longevity, vitality, and strength as we navigate our day-to-day life so we can fulfil the purpose for which we were created on earth before our time on this side of life expires. Help me especially to have an eternal perspective of both life and death, until death is finally defeated once and for all, in Jesus' name. Amen.

DAY SIX

FAITH

But let him ask in faith, with no doubting, for he who doubts is like a wave of the sea driven and tossed by the wind. (James 1:6 – NKJV).

I was recently on a program being interviewed and was asked this question, *"What is faith?"* My response, *"Faith is the technology we use to trade in order to bring the realities of another world into our world."* It is a simple answer but complex in its execution because, after 40+ years of being on earth, I have not seen the church replicate the full measure of faith as I have read in Scripture. Yet, it must for the church to become the glorious and radiant church Jesus returns a second time for.

Husbands, love your wives, just as Christ also loved the church and gave Himself for her, that He might sanctify and cleanse her with the washing of water by the word, that He might present her to Himself a glorious church, not having spot or wrinkle or any such thing, but that she should be

holy and without blemish. (Ephesians 5:25-27 - NKJV).

Personally, I don't believe Jesus is coming back for a church with homosexual and adulterous pastors and powerless pew members who are more churchgoers than disciples. I believe this word in Ephesians to be a prophetic announcement that will hint us to the times when we are approaching the closing of the age of time. Many Christians, in probing eschatological ideologies, see chaos as the informing event for heaven's intervention, but I am of a contrasting opinion. It is the glorious church that will signal the true end.

Faith has been truncated by many distractions and opposing forces to the point where it almost loses its validity in our modern-day cultures. Even the voice of God is not pursued as much as having a conversation with AI to determine how we move forward on certain issues. The voice of God is being drowned out by all the other competing voices, which is not a good thing. Faith requires that we hear what God says in order to obey and for there to be a manifestation of what was said. This is the divine partnership that was established from the very beginning, which we fell short of and which salvation addresses. Faith is a needed commodity in our day for God to remain relevant in our context. Otherwise, what we are building is another tower of babel reaching into the heavens in an attempt to make a name for ourselves independent of God.

Regardless of what we perceive is happening in our world today, we must not lose our foundation. If it requires us to be seen as queer and old-fashioned, we must maintain our quest to practice faith in order to bring the realities of heaven to earth. AI is a machine that is governed by the laws of our world. It has no consciousness of the world beyond this one and cannot influence our experience and knowledge of it.

"Talking to God" with the posture to obey His Word must never be a lost practice in our time. Don't lose your capacity to have faith in God, or you will lose your capacity to access God.

MEDITATION

Now faith is the substance of things hoped for, the evidence of things not seen. (Hebrews 11:1 - NKJV).

As we meditate on this Scripture, let's contemplate its meaning. Is faith the substance and evidence, or does it produce the substance and evidence? How does faith really work? Apostle James says if we doubt, we should not expect anything to happen when we exercise our faith. How do we stop ourselves from doubting when asking God for something seemingly impossible? What was the last time you prayed for someone to receive a miracle? Did it happen? How did that make you feel?

Spend about 15-30 minutes with this, then journal your thoughts as you come back from this meditation.

WHAT DID THE LORD SHOW YOU?

_____

_____

_____

_____

_____

_____

_____

_____

_____

_____

_____

_____

_____

WHAT DID THE LORD SAY TO YOU?

_____

_____

_____

_____

_____

_____

_____

_____

_____

_____

_____

_____

_____

_____

_____

_____

_____

_____

_____

_____

_____

_____

_____

_____

AFFIRMATION

I have faith to move mountains. I have faith to heal the sick and raise the dead. I have the faith to bring the realities of heaven to earth: *on earth as it is in heaven.* I am a conduit for the life of God to flow through me and out into the world.

PRAYER

Father, You gave us the authority to heal the sick and raise the dead. Jesus said that by virtue of our belief in Him, we would be able to do the same things He did and even greater things than these. Lord, I am believing You for greater. I believe that I have the authority over demonic entities, sickness, and death, that by the frequency of my voice, I can set captives free, give sight to the blind, speech to the dumb, and life to that which is dead. I speak life. I speak prosperity. I speak health. I speak miracles in my own life and in the lives of those connected to me. Out of my belly flows rivers of living water, providing hope and healing to the world. You have made me a light to shine in the darkness, in Jesus' name. May my faith produce that which is in Your heart and mind. Amen.

DAY SEVEN

ALL THINGS ARE YOURS

And whatever things you ask in prayer, believing, you will receive. (Matthew 21:22 – KJV).

All things are yours seem like wishful thinking when we apparently lack so much. In my quest for wealth, I found debts. The more I desire health, the more I battle that which is contradictory. It is hard sometimes to wrap my mind around the realities of Scripture and my actual experiences. They are seemingly as different as night and day, but I realize that faith establishes a reality that is not-yet, but is.

I cannot fathom the discrepancies between what I am believing God for and what I actually have in relation to having it all and lacking nothing. Maybe the conservatives are correct and we take some single verses of Scripture out of context to facilitate our own spiritual fantasies, but I cannot get out of my mind Jesus' words, "It is finished." There is a certain measure of finality to that statement that causes me to think that it already is, though experientially, it is not.

Let's take another look at the beginning. In Genesis 1, God creates. In Genesis 2, it says before there was anything there. There are two ways to quantify these two realities, but the one I love the most is that God creates as Spirit in Spirit, and man manifests in the physical reality. This explains why God allowed the man to "name" the animals. So, while the trees, plants, and shrubs were already spoken into existence, until the man was created, they hadn't manifested yet.

So, I have asked this question, *"When is a building real?"* Before it is constructed, it must be visualized. An architect takes some thoughts and ideas and creates the structural drawing of the entire building that, with the use of technology, can now be viewed in a 3D walk-through before the foundation is even laid. Is the building real at its conception or when the final coat of paint is applied?

If faith is the substance and the evidence, it means it brings our desires and requests into existence in a certain realm before they are manifested here in our physical reality. This does provide some clarity to this text:

Grace and peace be multiplied to you in the knowledge of God and of Jesus our Lord, as His divine power has given to us all things that pertain

to life and godliness, through the knowledge of Him who called us by glory and virtue. (2 Peter 1:2-3 - NKJV).

Essentially, you lack nothing, even though it has not all been manifested yet. All things are yours, according to Paul, though most of it is still in the realm of "not-yet." Be patient. Keep hope alive. Have faith. God is not through with you yet.

MEDITATION

But as it is written: "Eye has not seen, nor ear heard, nor have entered into the heart of man the things which God has prepared for those who love Him." (1 Corinthians 2:9 - NKJV).

This is a beautiful text to meditate on as it keeps us open to all divine possibilities. Sometimes we can hold too tightly to what we know that we leave very little room for God to reveal His hidden mysteries to us. If God came down in the cool of the day to fellowship with man, meaning, teach man all man needed to know, then that would have been interrupted by the fall. Can you imagine the eternity of information that man has not yet been privy to its revealing? (Read Job 38 to get a glimpse). Everything you have heard, seen, or imagined is not counted among the things God has prepared for you. Push your mind to see beyond what you already know. Allow God to reveal something new to you.

Spend about 15-30 minutes with this, then journal your thoughts as you come back from this meditation.

WHAT DID THE LORD SHOW YOU?

_____

_____

_____

_____

_____

_____

_____

_____

_____

_____

_____

_____

_____

_____

_____

_____

WHAT DID THE LORD SAY TO YOU?

_____

_____

_____

_____

_____

_____

_____

_____

_____

_____

_____

_____

_____

_____

_____

_____

_____

_____

_____

_____

_____

_____

AFFIRMATION

I have all things for life and godliness. I lack nothing. All that the Father has given to His Son, Jesus Christ, is also mine. I receive all that God has for me. I claim my birthright. I am seated with Christ in heavenly places. As He is, so am I in creation. I am made in the image and likeness of God.

PRAYER

Father, it is hard sometimes to fathom what You have accomplished on my behalf through Your Son, Jesus Christ. I struggle to see and hear beyond my immediate physical surroundings, but I speak to my eyes that they may open to see divine realities and possibilities. I speak to my ears that they be open to hear beyond what everyone else is hearing. I speak to my mind to conform to the mind of Christ so that it can be malleable to receive divine downloads and revelations. I speak to my heart to be open to Your visitations and gentle promptings. Holy Spirit, help my weaknesses and inadequacies in forming and developing an intimate relationship with You. I desire to know You and to walk with You now and for eternity. I present my body as a living sacrifice to You, Lord. May it be holy and acceptable to You. I position myself to encounter Your presence however You choose to reveal Yourself to me, in Jesus' name. Amen.

CONCLUSION

One of my deep-seated passions in the last decade or so of my faith walk is learning to hear God's voice. God has called for obedience from the very beginning of man (Adam), but obedience is impossible if we cannot hear God speaking. And God speaks in many different ways.

It is my intention to explore the different ways God speaks through these volumes, but feedback is paramount in continuing this series, so I implore you to send me some feedback on how this may or may not have resonated with you for the week you spent with it, and feel free to share any experiences or insights you may have received.

You can also visit my website here:
https://clevelandomcleish.com/

Let's take this journey of faith together!

The world is changing at a rapid pace, and if we are not careful, in a few years, many of heaven's protocols (spiritual disciplines and practices) will be overridden by technological advancements and the ever-evolving Babylonian systems of our day. There is a call for the remnant who will keep the unshakable values of God as relevant today as they have always been. Those values are Faith, Hope, and Love.